FOR THE KINGDOM OF GOD INSPIRATIONAL VERSE

Jessie M. R. LARMAN
Born Again Christian

Carnarvon
North Western Australia

Copyright © Jessie Larman 2021
First Edition: Carnarvon Art Studio 2021

All rights reserved. This book is copyright. Apart from any fair dealing for the purpose of private study, research, criticism or review, as permitted under the Copyright Act, no part of this book may be reproduced or transmitted in any form or by any means, electronic or mechanical, including photocopying, recording or by any information storage and retrieval systems without written permission from the publisher. Enquiries should be made to the publisher.

National Library of Australia

 A catalogue record for this book is available from the National Library of Australia

ISBN: 978-0-6450891-0-3 (paperback)
ISBN: 978-0-6450891-1-0 (ebook)

Distributed in Australia and Overseas by IngramSpark

Special thanks go to my friend
Jillian Dost
for her
invaluable help in reviewing
this book.

and to
John Blyth
for his Computer Help
****

CONTENTS

FOREWORD	1
One Little Prayer	3
Forgive me	4
Eternal Day	5
Dove of Peace	5
Your Children	6
Little One	7
Jesus is Coming	9
Deep in my Heart	10
Jesus Reigns	11
Dance & Sing	11
All The World Is Waking	12
Dew Fresh Morning	13
Yellow Flower	13
Show Me the Way	13
Wait - a - Minute	15

✝

All the Flowers	15
We Want to Give	16
Our Comforter	17
A Guardian Angel	18
Day is Here	19
Holy Spirit of Truth	20
Can I write a Song?	21
Spirit Of God	22
Be with Me	22
Omnipotent	24
Laugh & Sing	24
Time	25
Souls in Darkness	26
Awesome God	27
Love - Most Important	30
The Time Has Gone	31
A Silver Triangle	32

Show me the Way 32

To be set Free. 33

In Your Care 34

Saviour mine. 34

Seed of Love 35

Come Holy Spirit 36

The Answer 37

Heavenly Father 37

To-day 38

Our Ultimate Fate 38

This is the Day 38

Cage Bird 39

Holy Spirit the Spirit Of Jesus Christ 40

Wild Horses 41

In Quietness 42

Take the Darkness Away! 43

Feel His Love. 43

†

Intellect And God	44
Cheerfully!!!	45
Show That You Care	46
In the quietness of our minds	47
Share the Peace of the Lord	47
I've Forgotten	48
Fragrant Rose	49
Night is Here	50
Take My Hand.	51
The Kingdom of God.	53
Musical Instruments	54
Jesus	55
Creation Praising God	56

FOREWORD

I praise God for this book written only with the help of His Holy Spirit. I pray that who-ever reads these verses enjoy's them as much as I did in writing them.

Some of them show us the beauty of His world, the flowers He has given us, the beautiful creatures here on earth, - these have also been given for us to love and enjoy. Likewise our children, families, friends, these are all gifts God has given us to love and cherish. Remember they have been entrusted to us to care for.

Let us try to look at something of beauty each day - even just a leaf or a flower, everyone has something at hand to look at and wonder at.

Don't forget God's own book that He gave us to read and digest, it is still relevant to-day, in this present age, as it was at the time it was written.

I pray that God does bless you even as you turn the pages of this book.

Jessie.

LAMB. - JOHN:
Chapter 1. Verse 29.

The next day John saw Jesus coming towards Him and said, "Look, the Lamb of God, who takes away the sin of the world!"

One Little Prayer

Just one little prayer
to God up above.
Will open a channel
to His wonderful love.

Just one little prayer
earnest and true.
Will let you know
that He does love you.

Just one little prayer
in the depth of despair,
telling Jesus you're sorry
you will find God does care.

Just one little prayer
coming deep from your heart.
Ask His forgiveness
it's a wonderful start.

Forgive me

Forgive me for all the sins I've committed.
God in your goodness guide me now.
For years in the world of darkness I've been.
The light of your goodness I'd rarely seen.

But now I've been born of your Spirit.
The Spirit of Jesus - Your Son.
Your love overwhelms me each day as I live.
To God, Jesus and Holy Spirit - my body I give.

I give you my body now - healed and restored.
By Jesus Christ our most wonderful Lord.
I'm healed of deceases and wrong spirits now.
So it's time to go out in your Spirit and Sow.

Go out and sow the seed of true love,
Straight from God our Father above.
Jesus is with us each day as we live.
Holy Spirit of Jesus, Gods Love help us give.

Help us to give God's love, - to the poor.
The poor are the souls who have not opened the door.
Jesus our Lord is the one with the keys.
So come pray with me, go down on your knees.

Ask His forgiveness - He want's you to.
Then listen and do what He tell's you to do.
It's all in the Bible - God's wonderful Book.
Go on, open it up - just have a look.

Eternal Day

Thank you Jesus, coming for us.
Dying as you did on the cross.
Living in God's Kingdom supreme.
One day for us, may it be not a dream.
May we be there with you in glorious light.
Eternal day - no more night.

Dove of Peace.

Your Kingdom God was here on earth.
Even before Jesus was given birth.
The Souls of Man are your delight.
You want us pure in your sight.
Your Dove of peace you sent to Jesus.
Thank you for that Dove of Peace.
May your love for us

never cease.

Your Children

Your Children are not pets you know,
they are little Girls and Boys.
They are not things that you have found.
They are not - to be used as toys.

Each little Child has a heart you know.
That God Himself put there
and as the child begins to grow,
it fills with love, for Him to share.

As a Christian it's your job you know
to tell your child of Jesus.
Let Him know and understand -
that Jesus wants to please us.

Our Father in Heaven is God, you know,
so don't deny your Child.
Love him and tell him while he is young,
don't let him just run wild.

You can sing and rock him with love,
just as Mary did with her bundle of joy,
sent from God our Father in Heaven -
Who was - Jesus, His own little Boy.

So your children are not pets you know,
they are here to bring God Glory.
So hold them gently, sing to them
and tell them Jesus Story.

Little One

Little one sleeping there,
Tender Love Divine.
Little one Sleeping there,
Are you truly mine.

Has God given you to me,
Tender Love Divine?
Has God given you to me?
Yes, - You're truly mine.

LAMP. - LUKE:
Chapter 12.Verse 35.
Be dressed ready for service and keep your lamps burning.
***

(Readiness for the Lord's return.)

Jesus is Coming

Jesus is coming. He's coming one day.
Look forward to this and pray & pray.
Look to the Saviour of Glory above.
Repent now and praise Him, ask for His love.

Jesus is coming, He'll be here soon.
Will it be morning or afternoon.
None of us knows what time it will be
but He is sure coming for you and me.

Jesus is coming, so let us give praise.
Sing Hallelujah's let the roof raise.
Angels adore Him forever on high
and we shall all see Him bye and bye.

Jesus is coming, so get up and sing.
Give your best praise to Jesus our King.
God up above loves us right now,
He sent us His Spirit of love to show how.

Jesus is coming, praise God above.
With His Holy Spirit be filled with love
be happy and joyous, uplifted and free,
Jesus our Lord died for you and me.

Jesus is coming, He died on the cross
to save all us sinners, His life was no loss,
as He reigns now in Glory in Heaven you know,
so - tell of His story and His love He'll bestow.

Deep in my Heart

Deep in my heart there is a place,
that longs to look on Jesus face.
But I am not pure as pure can be.
So will His face - I ever see?

Yes, when I die and go home to Heaven.
My sins all washed seven times seven.
So then I shall be as pure as pure.
Then I shall see Jesus, sure as sure.

So come with me, be Born Again.
Open your heart - there is no shame;
In loving Jesus Christ our Lord.
Who by Angels is ever adored.

Jesus helps us here in this life.
His Holy Spirit helps us deal with strife.
He delivers us from all our foes.
As gently, His seeds of love He sows.

Deep in my heart there is a place,
waiting and waiting to see His face.
A face so beautiful, full of love.
Glory of Glory, shining down from above.

In Heaven above Gods Glory is there,
He sends it to earth for us to share.
So come and share with me to-day.
Open your heart - just start to pray.

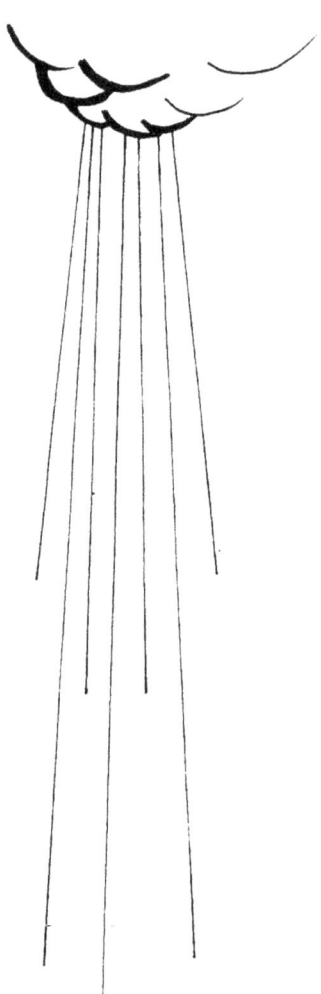

Jesus Reigns

Something wonderful has come to be,
Jesus is alive in me.
Imagine me with all God's power,
Not just now but every hour.

Imagine when the sun shines through.
Jesus is there for me and you.
Even when darkness begins to fall
Jesus still reigns over us all.

Dance & Sing

Dance & Sing the whole day
through.
There's never enough time for me
and you,
To praise our God up on high, Ruling
there but ever nigh.

* Share the Peace of the Lord *

ALL THE WORLD IS WAKING

All the world is waking, listen to the noise.
Soon you'll hear the voices of all the girls and boys.
Listen to the birds waking in the trees.
Smell the morning freshness, wafting on the breeze.

Jesus in your mercy look upon us all.
Waking in the mornings as the days unfurl.
Grant us peace, also love and joy each day.
For each woman, man, girl and boy.

Smell the freshness of the earth, once again to-day.
Open up your hearts to God, let Him hear you pray.
Thank Him for the joyful hours - to love, laugh, sing - enjoy the flowers.

All the world is waking, listen to the noise.
Soon you'll hear the voices of all the girls and boys.
Listen to the morning - waking all around.
Gods own creatures waking, to the morning sound.

Dew Fresh Morning

Water so clean so fresh so new,
Look at the mornings heavy dew.
Each plant covered and washed again,
Without even a drop of rain.

Walk on the dew fresh grass one morning.
A chance to meet without any warning.
Another soul just wanting to be,
Nearer my Lord - Nearer to Thee.

Yellow Flower

Beautiful little yellow flower.
Perfume exuding every hour.
Thank you God for such a gift.
Heaven sent healing for any rift.

Show Me the Way

Show me the way, oh! Saviour mine!
With your Great love - so Divine.
I long for your love, to be with Me
and that one great day your face I'll see.

WHEAT. - JOHN:
Chapter 12. Verse 24.

I tell you the truth, unless a grain of wheat falls to the ground and dies, it remains only a single seed. But if it dies, it produces many seeds.

***

(Spiritual Fruit - Christ's Death.)

Wait - a - Minute

God say's - wait - a minute.
This is warfare and you're in it.
Take your time but don't be slow.
Ask His help because you know,
Spiritual Warfare is the time,
You find God's love is divine.
He guides you through what-ever's there.
So in your heart don't despair.
Call on Jesus powerful name.
You only have yourself to blame
If in satan's world your host.
Instead of living with the Holy Ghost.

All the Flowers

All the flowers their faces lift
To the sky and never cry,
For anything us mortals need
Except -maybe for their seed,
To carry on their fruitfulness,
Of reproducing God's good work.
In making flowers of glorious hue
For the likes of Me and You.

We Want to Give

Sometimes when we want to give -
we want to give so much.
It hurts us that they do not know -
the love that they can have.

Jesus we want to bring them,
right into your Kingdom of love.
Just as you gently brought us to dwell,
in God's Kingdom by your dove.

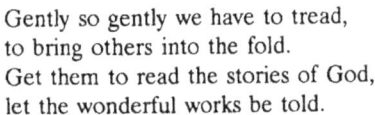

Gently so gently we have to tread,
to bring others into the fold.
Get them to read the stories of God,
let the wonderful works be told.

Let us tell them the story of Jesus,
Your Son who came there to earth.
Let us tell of His Holy Spirit,
who can give each one New Birth.

Let us bring them with love to the Kingdom.
God's Kingdom that is here right now.
Show them through Christians obedience,
The Y's and the Where's and the How.

That means to talk of Gods love
to the people who are not reborn.
Help them to know of God's Goodness.
Don't leave them sad and forlorn.

So tell them right now this minute -
of our Wonderful Saviour, named Jesus.
Don't be afraid to Witness to all.
Of God, Holy Spirit and Lord of your life - Christ Jesus.

So there you are Christians lets talk.
Say to the people out there -
God's Kingdom is here on earth now,
with a wealth of His love to share.

Our Comforter

Our Comforter is the - **Holy Spirit.**
Come, - my life, let's be in it.
With Jesus ruling and supreme,
Life can be a wonderful dream.

Forget your worries, forget your woes,
If it's possible get up on your toes.
Dance and sing, be merry and bright,
Live with Jesus now - lest you die tonight.

He is there so mighty and strong.
Try to do right, not what's wrong.
With God - and Jesus and the **Holy Spirit,**
Life's just great, when you live it!

A Guardian Angel

A Guardian Angel is sent for each Child that is born on earth for sure.
He guards the child as it grows, each day through-out it's life.

Wouldn't it be wonderful to see your Guardian Angel that God has sent.
Just believe that he is there - not quite in sight, for you to see.

We cannot see with earthly eyes the wonder of God's Heaven.
So when you accept Jesus into your heart odd things begin to happen.,

Even a child who knows Jesus, is a wonder to behold.
It is a little life filled with love even more than it's heart can hold.

Look at it's face, look into it's eyes. The child trusts you every day.
And that's the way Jesus wants us to be, full of love and trust and joy.

Our Guardian Angels must guard us, whether we are bad or good.
Lets acknowledge that we love Jesus, God our Father and His Holy Spirit.

A Guardian Angel sent from above - what a precious thing to know.
Little child dreaming there, with love you just seem to glow.

Day is Here

Morning has broken, the day is here.
Listen to the birds as they fly quite near.
The clouds are moving in the sky above.
May your heart just yearn and yearn full of love.

May your heart be filled with the love of Jesus.
Thank Him for each new day He sends us.
So let us walk in His Spirit for sure.
Every step of the way for evermore.

Let your heart skip & dance in the morning light.
The daytime is here, no-more night.
Sing for The Lord our God in Heaven.
Who forgives our sins seven times seven.

Look at the flowers, the trees, the leaves.
Could we have made anything such as these.
They are so beautiful standing there.
Go on and touch one - don't just stare.

Touch the softness of the petals to-day.
Feel them and the fragrance will stay
on your fingertips for a while.
Then smell them and you will gently smile.

When you smile with the love of The Lord.
You will join Angels as they praise our adored.
So morning has broken day is here.
Sing for joy-knowing Jesus is near.

Holy Spirit of Truth

Holy Spirit of Truth
Please in me abide.
Be in me forever
and be by my side.
Help me to speak,
just as Jesus would
and sing like His Angels
if only could.

Can I write a Song?

How can I write a song from my heart?
I don't even know where to start -
to praise my Lord in Heaven above.
Tell me how do I start to talk about love.

I love you Jesus seems the best I can say.
I love you now God - and every day.
But how can I tell you these things in my heart.
Holy Spirit you're here, please help me to start.

Let me start to say I care, yes - I care.
But I have so much love that I want to share.
So how can I tell you Jesus - you see,
as I am only a very - humble me.

I don't reckon I rate much on a scale of ten.
But I love you much more than just now and then.
Jesus I love you day after day - after day.
God's Holy Spirit is showing me the way!

So may-be I can write a song from my heart,
if only your Spirit will guide me to start.
Then a song will come forth glorious and new
and Jesus I'll spend ever,more loving you.

SPIRIT OF GOD

Spirit of God wondrous light.
May I receive your Spirit's sight.
Jesus is Lord of my life right now,
He's changed it around, My! and How!

Once in the darkness I failed to see
The world of God's Spirit around me.
Now I'm reborn, a Child of God,
Forever while I walk this sod.

This sod, this earth, this realm.
Holy Spirit you overwhelm.
But it is so wonderful having you here,
The earthly world now holds no fear.

God is love through and through.
Jesus God's Son we Worship You.
For sending your Spirit to us on earth.
When we receive our Rebirth.

Be with Me

Holy Spirit be with me,
Forever more and we shall see,
The marvellous things you can achieve
When we are given God's Reprieve!

SWORD. - HEBREWS:
Chapter 4. Verse 12.

For the Word of GOD is living and active. Sharper than any double-edged sword, it penetrates even to dividing Soul and Spirit, Joints and Marrow; it judges the thoughts and attitudes of the heart.

***

(Spiritual weapons, Power of the Word.)

Omnipotent

The Power of God Omnipotent and True,
is ever there for me and you.
Step out in faith and you will see most wondrous things,
that can ever be.
For God is Almighty.
God is Love.
He Reigns Forever.
Here and above.

Laugh & Sing

Let us laugh and let us sing.
Praises to our Heavenly King.
Here on earth and in Heaven above.
He can fill us with His love.

TIME

There is NO TIME -
days merge into one another.
Nights come and go them too into one another.

Eternity is FOR EVER -
days and nights merging as one.
Love with God is eternal, us merging into His Son.

We live in the light, of The Lord Jesus Christ.
Coming to God through His name.
Being filled with the Spirit of Jesus, who is - His Holy Ghost.

Merging together as one.
Father, Son & Holy Spirit.
United forever to be -
merging and moving, enveloping, breaking our sin.

There is no time on earth to waste with trivial things.
To-day, tomorrow, yesterday - Yes - TIME itself has wings.
Merge with The Lord Jesus to-day, invite Him into your heart.
Merge with the past, present & future.
For Eternity - Jesus is the only start.

There is no time to delay.
Love conquers all in the world.
Love is eternal, love is The Lord. Merge into timeless love, with the Adored.

Souls in Darkness

For all those poor Souls in darkness God
we pray to you to-day.
Let them know that you are real.
Help them to kneel and pray.

Of all people on earth who pray,
please show them that Jesus is Lord.
Let them know that He is King
He is your own Adored.

All in sin and sickness, in darkness,
oppressed and sad.
Lead them to your Kingdom God,
Where they will become so glad.

Those in the streets round about,
those in their prisons shut in -
Let them open the doors that keep them there.
Forgive them all their sin.

Show them that Jesus can set them free -
Free as the birds in the air.
Let them be born of your Spirit of love.
With Jesus our Lord let them share.

Help us to show the unsaved the way.
Holy Spirit, help us to pray - for all lost in the world,
For our brothers, our sisters, our families, our friends.
Then may the wonderful Kingdom of Jesus - to them be
unfurled.

Awesome God

We serve an Awesome God.
Powerful and Mighty.
Full of justice and Love.
He is God Almighty.

Put away your trivial things.
Praise His name on high.
Praise Him, Son & Holy Spirit.
So that You don't die.

Thank Him for your life,
for your everyday living.
Come to God in Prayer
Stop your awful sinning.

He is the God of Love.
Merciful and True.
Enter into His Kingdom.
Know His love for you.

Jesus came to save us.
Take Him at His word.
God our Father in Heaven
Is worthy to be served.

We serve an Awesome God.
Mighty and true.
Get down on your knees and Pray.
Don't let satan have you.

Repent of your sins,
Come into God's light,
Have Jesus Christ as your Lord.
Do you know it is your right.

CROWN - I CORINTHIANS:
Chapter 9. Verse 25.

Everyone who competes in the games goes into strict training. They do it for a crown that will not last; but we do it to get a crown that will last forever.

(Spiritual Striving- Spiritual Crowns.)

In Glory with Jesus

The day is coming it is drawing nigh.
When surely all of us will have to die.
But don't be sorry and don't be sad.
Jesus is there - so laugh be glad.

Glad you should be when it's time to die.
As long as your life was not one big lie.
So think of Jesus so loving and sweet.
Calm yourself down and lay at His feet.

He died on the cross that we might be saved.
So don't be frightened of the grave.
It's only your body and bones will be there.
Your soul and your spirit will be elsewhere.

Above the clouds in glory with Jesus -
Glowing with beauty and love for us -
are Angels, aglow with a wonderful light.
Singing for-ever and dressed in white.

Love - Most Important

Love is the most important thing.
Open your heart let it come in.
Only when you let love into your heart,
can you truly make a fresh start.

Then you can learn to love your brother,
Christian people should love each other.
Not just now but day after day,
then together with Jesus learn to pray.

Give your Sister in Christ a smile,
you may not see her for a while.
Don't let hate and misery and greed
be in you or you can't intercede.

Love is the important thing in life
not anger, hate, worry and strife.
So love each other as Jesus loves you.
Get on with the work He gives you to do.

Don't look to the left then to the right.
Keep Jesus always in your sight.
He will bless you as only He can.
When you help Him carry out His plan.

Don't keep asking for worthless things.
Soar to heavenly places as on wings.
Love, Peace, Joy and Grace
are the blessings that win the race.

Look at each other - stop the doubt.
Don't try to catch each other out.
We are not to judge our Sisters & Brothers.
Jesus loves each one - as much as the others.

The Time Has Gone

The time has gone the years have flown.
Also some of the family and friends I've known.
Why didn't I say the things I should
Why was my heart like a block of wood.

Now I am sorry the things I can see
Sorry that I wasn't the real me.
So now it's too late and I'm far away,
for those I can't see, - At least I can pray.

Last time I saw her - one soul so dear - was getting old,
I could only hold her near.
She wasn't quite sure if it was me,
- the one she used to sit on her knee.

The time has gone the years have flown.
She was a dear one that I had known.
Why didn't I keep in touch much more,
it's too late now and she's old and sore.

Her bones are old and her hair is grey
but she was the one that taught me to pray.
She used to tell me that Jesus was real,
that we must be good - not swear and steal.

She told me God loves us just as we are,
she taught me to look for that wonderful star.
To me she seemed old even when I was young
My Aunt was a very - very dear one.

A Silver Triangle

A Silver Triangle appeared to me.
It was to represent the Trinity.
God the Father, God the Son.
God the Spirit, Three in One.

Each one Equal standing firm,
in the Triangle glowing there.
Three sides strong as each could be,
A Good strong firm Trinity.

Divided, a Triangle cannot stand.
So come along take God's hand.
Share in His Glory - yes you and me.
It is for Us, God's Trinity.

The Truth of the Trinity is hard to take.
But God above really did make -
Himself, Holy Spirit and Jesus His Son.
All in together, Separate but One.

Show me the Way

Show me the way oh! Saviour mine.
With your Great Love so Divine.
I long for your love to be with me and
that one great day your face I'll see.

To be set Free.

I've been set free to Worship the Lord.
Our King of love for ever adored.
Holy Spirit you love Him so.
Teach me now, till into Heaven I go.
To be there with Jesus our Saviour above.
Filled ever-more with His glorious Love.

A love so big so strong so true.
Waiting there-also especially for you.
So don't sit and dream of what might be.
God really is there for you and me.
Let us rise in the mornings and sing His praise.
Look forward now to those Heavenly days.

Here on earth you can have the Lord's love.
God sent His Holy Spirit, represented by the dove.
If you open your heart to let Jesus in -
He will take away your fear and your sin.
Then after that invite His Holy Spirit too
To dwell in Him and He in you.

Then you will be set free to worship The Lord,
Jesus Christ our King, who is also, -by Angels adored.
God sends His Angels to minister to us.
They are so quiet, never making a fuss
and they love The Lord truly as surely we must.
So in God, Jesus -God's Son and The Holy Spirit ,let's put our trust.

In Your Care

In Your loving care I stand,
You are sitting at God's right hand.
I am not fit to stand and stare.
Jesus, it's wonderful to know you're there.

You keep me safe by night and day.
Morning and night you let me Pray.
I need your love as long as I live
and my whole self is what I give.

I give you myself that's what you need,
to deliver me from want and greed.
May you fill my being with your wondrous love,
Pouring it down from up above.

Saviour mine.

Little candle glowing bright,
Lighting up the darkest night.
Through my tears I see your glow.
Your flame starts to flicker and then to grow.

My tears I shed are not for you.
You are so bright and strong and true.
I am so weak in mind and body,
against your glory I feel so shoddy.

Maybe one day I'll be so strong,
Tell me Jesus that I'm not wrong,
To want your love so divine
and as Saviour you are mine.

Seed of Love

Have you ever felt the Glory of The Lord?
Have you ever felt oneness with The Adored?
If you have you are privileged indeed -
Because in you God has truly planted His Seed.

So tend and nurture this seed of love.
Given you through Jesus Christ from above.
Who is with our Father God in Heaven.
Who forgives our sins Seven times seven.

Treasure always the Blessings he gives.
Then live the life that God wants us to live.
Go out in power - proclaim His name.
Your life will certainly not be tame.

As you walk with Jesus Christ as Lord.
People will notice your gifts that are stored.
Gifts stored in your heart of peace & joy,
They are there for every girl and boy.

So pass on the love Jesus has given you.
Get up and to out there's lots to do.
Sing and dance, join in the Godly fun.
Pick up His cross and run, run, run.

Go to the people tell them you care.
The Glory of God is not a snare.
It sets you free from earthly things:
Let your Soul soar until it sings.

If you have never felt the Glory of The Lord.
Tell God you love Jesus He is your adored.
Ask Jesus to come right into your heart.
His Glory will then come - what a wonderful new start.

Come Holy Spirit

Come Holy Spirit
Guide us to-day.
Come Holy Spirit,
Teach us to pray.

Teach us to pray.
Guide us for sure.
Open our hearts,
now and evermore.

Show us God's Glory
the wonder of Ages.
Let all know the Story
through the Bible Pages.

The story of Jesus
who came down to earth.
The story of Jesus
Who gives us new birth.

Come Holy Spirit
teach us to-day.
Guide us and lead us.
Please show us the way.

The Answer

Dear God my head is going round and round.
The answer for me I still have not found,
What shall I do for the rest of the day?
NO - I can't go on, I shall have to pray!

Thank you God for being here.

Heavenly Father

Heavenly Father up above fill us please with your love.

Love to share with one another, each Christian Sister also Brother.

Let us help each other now, please Lord Jesus show us how.

Guide our hands and our feet, let our eyes in your love meet.

Fill us with your Heavenly power, day by day, hour by hour.

Grant us peace and love and joy, till we're with you bye and bye.

To-day

To-day is a new day.
Only just born.
But forgive me God.
I missed the Dawn.

Our Ultimate Fate

Jesus your power is mighty and great.
We pray that Heaven is our ultimate fate.
To be with you and our Father there.
With your Holy Spirit too, we'll have joy to spare.

This is the Day

This is the Day that the Lord has made.
Come He say's don't be afraid.
Laugh and play, sing and pray.
Why not have a glorious day!

CAGE BIRD

Cocky in a cage spreading your wings out wide.
Sitting on your perch, watching the world outside.
You poor old thing just longing to fly,
waiting to take off - to sail through the sky.

Why do people shut you in and lock the door?
It should be open wide for evermore!
So that you can come and go as you please.
With never a fear, to fly back & forth, in comparative ease.

But we are like Cockies trapped in a cage.
Our Spirit shut in as we grow old with age.
The door of our body is our heart you know.
We need to open our heart to Jesus to let His love flow.

Then like a bird on the wing our own Spirit can fly.
To the heavenly places - even past the sky.
Into eternity to our God who is here - and above,
Who fills our hearts with His wondrous love.

A love so filling - a love so divine.
Open the door now, it's yours and it's mine.
Don't sit in the dark waiting for ever.
Once Jesus is with you - He'll leave you never.

Cage birds sit on their perch all day.
They can never learn - what it's like to pray.
But we can enter the realms up above
and soar like Eagles to a place full of love.

Praise you Jesus, praise God on high.
So far away but - ever nigh.
Lets open that cage door of our heart,
That really is a good place to start.

HOLY SPIRIT the SPIRIT OF JESUS CHRIST

Spirit of the Living Lord,
be with me to-day.
Spirit of the Living Lord
help me learn to pray.

Holy Spirit full of love.
You are the Spirit of Jesus.
Only by God's heavenly grace,
does He send you to fill us.

Spirit of the Living Lord,
You are The Holy Ghost.
Our bodies are your temple,
You are - our Divine Host.

Holy Ghost, Living Lord,
grant us grace to-day.
Mercy too, we really need,
as our prayers we pray.

So, Spirit of The Living Lord,
be with me to-day.
Spirit of the Living Lord,
help me learn to pray.

Wild Horses

Wild as the wind the horses run.
Tossing and neighing in the sun.
God above has given us these.
Beautiful creatures - run in the breeze.

Toss your manes - hold your heads high.
Look to your Maker in the sky.
When you stand still surely you know,
God your Maker loves you so.

Sometimes, when you stand so still,
It's as though you really know His will.
You are obedient standing there.
Even though you look and stare.

What do you think in your beautiful head?
God has clothed you and you are fed.
He gave the grass to grow for you.
The land for you to run through.

So run my beauty - wild and free,
Ever more - for God gave you to me,
To love and appreciate, Beauty of God.
Run wild one, where no man's trod.

In Quietness

In quietness and confidence I come to you Lord.
I praise you and thank you, you are my adored.
Each morning I praise you and thank you too
and pray that your will is what I want to do.
To do your work is an honour for me.
Your Love abounds so full and free,
it envelopes me when to God I pray
and your angels keep me safe day by day.
Your Holy Spirit is with me for sure.
My heart held the key, Jesus opened the door.
I let Him come in to take hold of my life.
Now you are mine instead of trouble and strife.
You saved me from sin as you died on the cross.
Your death to your friends was a terrible loss but Jesus, you came back from the grave
for sinners like me - you came back to save,
to take us where no mortal has trod, or can.
Home to Heaven with your Wonderful I AM.
WHO IS - GOD ABOVE - GOD OF LOVE - GOD OF WONDER - OF HOPE AND JOY - GOD - WHO CASTS MY SIN ASUNDER!.
By His Son Jesus Christ who came into my heart, I pray now that we never part.
Jesus I need you in my heart right now.
Through your Holy Spirit for ever show me how.
So that in quietness and confidence I can pray.
In love and reverence through Jesus to you my GOD each day.

Take the Darkness Away!

Please let the dark go away.
May I sing to you to-day.
Please may I praise you,
Jesus my Lord.

Take the darkness away.
Please love me to-day.
Let me Praise your Holy Name,
Jesus my Lord.

Darkness has now flown away.
Thank you now I can pray.
To my Saviour above
Jesus my Lord.

Feel His Love

Come along take my hand
let us run along the sand.
Feel the wet beneath your feet
think of Jesus on the mercy seat.
Run. run. run along the beach
Jesus is never out of reach.
Stop and feel He presence there,
look - feel His presence everywhere.
In the light and in the shade,
even in the water as you wade.
Feel His presence - feel His love
here on earth and up above.

INTELLECT AND GOD

I saw a row of electric light bulbs standing there,
the first one very small about 5w next 15w then 30w on to 40,50,60 up
to 70watt, yes you can go higher but up to 70w was the highest I saw.

Now sitting there, on their own waiting for light, is much the same as mans
plight, we sit around but cannot see - God is the light for you and me.
But we have to plug into that invisible power, not just once, not just each
day but hour by hour.

For the brightness to shine from the electric globes they must be plugged
into the source of power, then they light up with a wonder full glow.

Just as people can when God they know.

Each globe receives the right amount of power, too much would make the
small one burst, not enough and the large would be dim, as with people
and their minds, i.e. their intellect, it lets the right amount in.

So we can all be together to pray to God and each receive his just
reward. Then together we make a shining array as we praise Jesus our Lord
each day.

So the lesson we learn is simple and true
God loves me and He also loves you.
However bright we are in our mind,
Jesus our Lord is so very kind,
He gives us all the chance to be -
at last with God in eternity.

CHEERFULLY!!!

Cheerfully, cheerfully do God's work.
Cheerfully, cheerfully please don't shirk.
Don't look to the left then, to the right.
Just keep straight on with all your might.

The Word of the Lord is true for sure.
It will stand now and for evermore.
So rest in His Spirit, just do His will.
GO - Cheerfully, cheerfully don't stand still.

Out in the world people are waiting to see,
Christians like you and Christians like me.
Cheerfully, doing our daily tasks.
So, cheerfully, answer whatever- anyone asks.

Give God the Glory, give God the praise.
Tell Him you love Him through all of your days.,
Jesus will bless you in your work each day.
Especially if sometimes you cheerfully pray.!!!

Show That You Care

*Full of compassion we need to be
for lost people out there in the world.
They need to be born of the Spirit of God
Through Jesus Christ our Lord.*

*This is a sign that we Christians care,
as we tend these people each day.
The love and joy we have in the Lord,
we must share with them and pray.*

*We can pray in private to God,
through Jesus His Son our Lord.
Praise Him that He has chosen you
to be one of His own adored.*

*Then after you've praised Him
and thanked Him for this,
pray that lost Brothers and Sisters,
may come to know His wonderful bliss.*

*To be happy and blissful
and joyous each day,
is a wonderful way
to teach others to pray.*

*So show your compassion for others,
grieve that they come to the Lord.
Pray that they ask His forgiveness.
Maybe, - to-day they'll be Reborn!.*

In the quietness of our minds

In the quietness of our minds God,
We feel your wonderful presence.
In the quietness of our minds God,
Let us feel your constant love.

In the quietness of our minds God,
Let us feel that we can praise you.
In the quietness of our minds God,
May we give our-selves to you.

Share the Peace of the LORD

It was a wonderful feeling Lord God,
to feel your love envelope me with the arms of my Christian Brother.
To feel so safe and pure and free.
Your love just flowed from one to the other.
Such a wonderful embrace is something to treasure,,
It is beyond words - Love without Measure.

Share the Peace of the Lord.

I've Forgotten

In my frustration I cry to you.
The word I've forgotten, oh! what shall I do?
I was asked to pray and ask you for this-
Special request, this special wish.

Please bless the family I'm praying for.
Give them your love and show them the door.
Truly they love you God you know.
May they Open that door, let it be so.

Let them love each other as families should.
Just as you and Jesus would.
May their children grow in love for you.
And you keep them all safe, whatever they do.

In my frustration I cry to you.
The word I've forgotten, oh! what shall I do?
But you know the word that I should speak.
Please bless the family, although I am weak.

Thank you Jesus for listening to me.
Asking help for that............family.
Your Will, will be done, I pray.
As I am asking this through your Son today.

Fragrant Rose

Dear God I'm thinking of that flower.
Ever fragrant in every hour.
The wonders of this Universe
makes one want to write a verse.
The delicate softness of the petals
Against the hardness of different metals.

To touch a Rose is a wonderful thing
Man made metals - no real pleasure bring.
But to touch and smell a dew fresh Rose,
Is a pleasure few of us really knows.

To touch and feel your wonderful world,
Especially the Petals so curiously curled.
What a priceless treasure the Rose must be,
I pray they'll be there in eternity!

Thank you GOD for being Here!

Night is Here

The day has gone the night is here,
Christians though have nothing to fear.
Born of the spirit of Jesus above,
rest in His precious gracious love.

Sleep in peace the whole night through.
Angels are there for me and you.
God in His Heaven adores all His flock.
So close your eyes, don't look at the clock.

If you wake in the night, never take fright.
Remember we are Sons of Light.
Rejoice in comfort as on your bed you lay.
Turn to Jesus, ask Him to help you pray.

While you are praying and half asleep.
God may just have a little peep.
At you His child in His Kingdom of love.
As He watches over you from above.

Angels adore Him and so should we.
And Jesus dear face we should long to see.
So sleep and rest in peace on your bed.
As God's Angels hover over-head.

God in His Wisdom gives us grace.
And each in His Kingdom has a place.
A place so special in His heart.
Remember He loved you from the very start.

The day has gone the night is here.
Christians though have nothing to fear.
Born of the spirit of Jesus above.
Rest in His precious gracious love.

Take My Hand.

Jesus said 'Take My Hand'
Through the Depth and Breadth of the Land.
Come with Me and you shall be free.
Just as I was at thirty - three.

To be with My Father I rose to Glory.
So that everyone might know my Story.
From Babe in a Manager I grew to a Man.
So that everyone knows God's Heavenly Plan.

There is a love so Great and Strong.
That comes from God and is never wrong.
So - 'Take My Hand' come and see.
It's your's as well - for Eternity.-

Thank you God for being here!

CROSS. - LUKE:
Chapter 9. Verse 23.

Then He said to them all:
"If anyone would come after Me, he must deny himself and take up his cross daily and follow me."

The Kingdom of God.

This is my world the Kingdom of God.
This is my world filled with His love.
The mist of time now holds at bay
His Glory of Glories - till that Great Day.

This is my world with Jesus as Lord.
This is my world with all gifts stored.
The mist holds the treasures we cannot see.
But God say's they're there for you and me.

This is my world of the Holy Spirit.
This is my world as I walk in it.
The mist let's the Spirit of Jesus shine through.
So wonderful, glorious for me and for you.

This is my world come share it with me.
This is my world peep in now and see.
The mist you may part for Gods Spirit to flow.
Right into your life so that Jesus you'll know.

Musical Instruments

Tambourines & Harps play their tune so well.
Listen to the music as it starts to lull and swell.
Each Instrument has it's part to play in the tune.
But we must be obedient to let the music bloom.

Like a flower that opens petals to the sky,
Instruments play their part, as in our hands they lie.
Music enfolds as we touch the strings with love.
Our hearts, with the instruments, then speak to The Lord above.

Organ and piano, guitar and other things,
Open up with music, each one to God then sings.
Every instrument has a voice, so different from each other.
Just as we have vocal cords, to sing in harmony with our brother.

God just loves to hear your voice, singing full of love.
The notes of song just drifting upwards, upwards to above.
So play your instrument with all your soul and heart,
Sing if you can with gusto- or maybe quietness to start.

Sing out your love song to The Lord of Lords.
Jesus Christ our saviour who Heaven & Earth adores.
Instruments, speak and sing together in tune.
Orchestra's, Flutes, Cello, Harmonica's, Violins even Bassoons.

Varied and colourful, different sizes and shapes.
It dosn't much matter so long as music it makes.
Gentle so gentle the tunes can drift, like the morning breeze.
Imagine playing an instrument such as one of these.

Jesus

Jesus is wonderful,
Jesus is King!
Jesus was not just a wild fling!
Jesus is love and peace on earth.
Jesus came in a miraculous Birth.

Jesus the baby grew to a Man.
And loves us all as much as He can.
He sits in Heaven with God His Father.
Waiting for us, in the Here-after.

JESUS IS LORD

Creation Praising God

Have you watched all Creation praising God on high.
Have you heard the rustle of the leaves on the trees.
Have you watched the grass sway back and forth with a sigh.
Have you ever heard the birds sing as they fly in the breeze?

Have you received Him into your heart - to be reborn.
Have you asked Jesus into your life, into your body.
Have you given Him your life, for Him to reform.
Have you told Him you care, have you given Him your body?.

Listen, can you hear Creation praising God on high.
Listen, can you hear the rustle of the leaves on the trees.
Listen, can you see the grass sway back and forth - with a sigh.
Listen, can you hear the birds sing as they fly in the breeze?.

If you are quiet and care to look, all these things you will see.
If you are quiet and care to listen, all these things you will hear.
If you are quiet and as quiet as you can be -
Then you will know that Gods Kingdom is very, very near.

ALPHA & OMEGA.
Revelation: Chapter 22. Verse 13.

I am the Alpha and the Omega, the First and the Last,
the Beginning and the End.

www.ingramcontent.com/pod-product-compliance
Lightning Source LLC
Chambersburg PA
CBHW071415290426
44108CB00014B/1827